© *Pino González*

## About the Author

Silvia Rodríguez (Las Palmas de Gran Canaria, 1970) graduated in Translation and Interpreting Studies at the University of Granada (Spain) and has published various poetry collections such as *Rojo Caramelo* (Toffee Red), *El Ojo de Londres* (The London Eye), *Casa Banana* (Banana House), *Shatabdi Express, Bloc de Notas (Notebook) and Provincia de Dolor* (Province of Pain) in the Canary Islands; *Departamento en Quito* (Apartment in Quito) in Madrid; *Ciudad Calima* (Sea-Mist City) and *Padresueño* (DreamFather) in Granada; *Las princesas no tienen nombre* (Princesses don't have names) in Seville; *Marabulla* (Forfeits) in Navarra (International Poetry Prize *María del Villar* 2018); a second edition in *Nectarina Editorial-Colección Libellus*, 2021, The Canary Islands; a third edition in the collection "*Rosa de los Vientos*" in *Palabrava*, Santa Fe, the Republic of Argentina.

## About the Translator

Margaret Hart Robertson (Dundee, Scotland:1954) is a happily retired ex-Senior Lecturer at the University of Las Palmas de Gran Canaria's Faculty of Translation and Interpreting and ex-Director of the Master and Doctorate Courses in Responsible Tourism in the same establishment.

She has worked in many fields in interpreting and safeguarding identity and intangible heritage, from UN Global Geoparks in Ecuador to her work as an interpreter for UNWOMEN and other official bodies.

# Forfeits

# Silvia Rodríguez

## Forfeits

Olympia Publishers
*London*

www.olympiapublishers.com
OLYMPIA PAPERBACK EDITION

Copyright © Silvia Rodríguez 2023

The right of Silvia Rodríguez to be identified as author of this work has been asserted in accordance with sections 77 and 78 of the Copyright, Designs and Patents Act 1988.

**All Rights Reserved**

No reproduction, copy or transmission of this publication may be made without written permission.
No paragraph of this publication may be reproduced, copied or transmitted save with the written permission of the publisher, or in accordance with the provisions of the Copyright Act 1956 (as amended). The cover photo (1977) is copyright of the author's mother, María del Pino González Gil. English translation copyright: Margaret Hart Robertson and Silvia Rodríguez.

Any person who commits any unauthorised act in relation to this publication may be liable to criminal prosecution and civil claims for damage.

A CIP catalogue record for this title is available from the British Library.

ISBN: 978-1-80074-865-1

This is a work of fiction.
Names, characters, places and incidents originate from the writer's imagination. Any resemblance to actual persons, living or dead, is purely coincidental.

First Published in 2023

Olympia Publishers
Tallis House
2 Tallis Street
London
EC4Y 0AB

Printed in Great Britain

# Dedication

For María del Pino González Gil, my mother, who gifted us the future.

# Acknowledgements

Thanks to my translator, Margaret Hart Robertson and to my permanent source of inspiration in my life, Pedro Flores. And to Nicola Evans for the introduction to Olympia.

# PROLOGUE

*Take a rose thorn
and we will seal it with blood*

— Silvia Rodríguez

Hypocrite reader – my semblance – my brother!

I wish to apologise in advance because this text attempts (and fails, much to my despair) to explain just why I am so bowled over by this work of Silvia's. From the first time I read it, it seemed her most mature work, most rounded and most complete. I am touched by her tenderness and amused by her irony. Her sarcastic remarks take me by surprise, and I hurt with the pain that still persists after beautiful jests or a happy verse. Silvia has her own very distinct voice, not just in women's poetry, that commonplace category, but rather in poetry with a capital "P". I am surprised and intrigued by her ironic nostalgia, how she plays with time, how she creates images, her used objects. Her poetry keeps me awake. It leaves me with a lasting hangover like a *cubalibre* made with rough rum. But, to the heart of the matter...

Every collection of poems is, somehow or other, a way of coming to terms with the past. Sometimes, even with the future. Maurice Blanchot says that "(...) *the poetic work is only a work when it becomes intimacy revealed by someone who writes to someone who reads it.*" Forfeits (*Marabulla*) is right now Silvia Rodríguez´s latest collection and it is a bright shop window full of intimacies revealed, a look back from maturity on childhood and the false innocence of the Arcadia we inhabit during childhood. It invites us to play with her in the game of Forfeits, to feel our way around the dark corners and identify people and things, as she explained when she first presented her book. *"To learn to touch things, to give them names again (…) to interpret, in short, our dreams and our nightmares,"* as Juan Carlos Rodríguez said of a book by Javier Egea. This is what Silvia does: she names the things she touches, things that are picked out in a new light by her naming them. And the poet from Gran Canaria travels back in her time to tell the story of a trip through a childhood that is no longer hers and so she recreates it, invents it, remembers it. *"That bitter taste left by a trip! / Monotonous and small the world today, yesterday/Tomorrow, in hindsight, it will conjure up another image,"* was how Baudelaire put it. And this is the trip upon which Silvia embarks, running the risk of knowing, of understanding. And that risk is real: words have their owners, as Lewis Carroll reminds us in Alice… And to contravene that norm brings various dangers: *a guard will come/ he will tell us we are crazy/ and he will handcuff our nostalgia*, is how Silvia puts it. Because childhood is not a game, and if it were, it would be Blind Man's Bluff or Forfeits where we have to grope around in the darkness to identify the traces of pain that allow us to find ourselves, identify ourselves: *I was a foreigner with no language/ and a hump full of unknowns* is how Silvia identifies herself because, in the end we travel the world with our *ragged crew*, a universe where we are always foreigners in a remote country with no language. With no language or, Freudian style, in the absence of language. For that reason, we can only dialogue sometimes in silence, in the silence of absence: *now papá/ you are that bird I remember/ and I am still that little girl/ but your pain is too much/ for me to handle.* And so, she creates a new language; a language that allows her to retrieve a character that lives in her memory, a kind of Captain Grant rescued from the island of memory, on the only stage where it is possible for the subconscious to wander at will. And Silvia walks along the paths of time past, plays the games of the past, sails over water-tanks and visits places within her heart in a kind of flashback architecture that she builds for herself. *"Yes, for me, desert, my youth flowers!"* says Herodias in Mallarmé's work. So, the childhood that she creates with her new language becomes a permanent today for the poet, a retrieval, not exempt of pain, of lost territory, a re-belonging. *"Genius is our childhood retrieved at will"* – again, the words of Baudelaire. In a marvellous aporia, Silvia boldly retrieves the future of her past: *while you took our photo/ and you gifted us the future.* And we are her readers, her guests invited to wander around her private space, where private overlaps public in language, in poetry. If Heidegger talked about language as the "house we live in", Silvia Rodríguez gives us a tour, a trip around that house, where the house she lives in is her own language without language: its silences, its images, the photos in black and white. She welcomes us into the secret space she makes public: *at the entrance there were two flowerpots/ with blue hortensias/ that smelt of other times.* But as Vázquez Montalbán said of Gil de Biedma, *"He taught the later poet to place himself where he could observe the poetic subject and narrate it according to the ethical rhythm of nostalgia."* So does Silvia, with that eternal smile of hers. She builds brief poems with the clear-cut effectiveness with which Gropius constructs his buildings: clearly defined lines with no unnecessary adornment, formal clarity that strips the candour of the cruellest nostalgia even further if possible. She never complains, but her memory, that flits back between the past and the present, emits pain, a daily ache, with its diamond-cutting clarity, going back like Herodias, revisiting childhood: *everything is sticky with a sad substance/ that leaves its dark trace/ of somebody disintegrating.*

When we enter in the game of Forfeits (*Marabulla*) as we are invited to by the poet, we make a pact and seal it with blood, pricking our fingers with a rose-thorn, and we agree to breathe slowly, silently, to walk cautiously and to wish that the Indian laurel may never die because:

*That was a place to return to*
*a beautiful tree under which we grew*
*wildly free*

Silvia Rodríguez makes her poetic voice heard again with the ethical rhythm of the nostalgia of used objects. Brecht would have liked it. Don't miss out on her.

— Ángel Collado

I celebrate myself, and sing myself
And what I assume you shall assume,
For every atom belonging to me as good belongs to you

— Walt Whitman


And what if these two stars
small twins sparkling were the two tiny eyes
wicked harassing evil of god

— Idea Vilariño


Perhaps death is an inexistent house
a cartoon door that
opens onto the void and a fleeting vertigo

— Pedro Flores

# The Farm

We loved to watch snails
hide among the daisies
breakfast fresh cow's milk

we would go to the well
and sail over the water-tank
to a remote country

they were days of games
and nights of peace

# Baby Bird

I breathe like the baby bird
that we cared for some days
for its little broken leg

we gave it apples
and healed its wound
but it needed to fly to live

now papá
you are the bird I remember
and I am still that little girl
but your pain is too much
for me to handle

# The Pond

By day it is a flat mass of green
with a branch or two floating on top
and shadowy tadpoles below the murky surface

at dusk, the frogs emerge
croaking as if coming up for air
after lurking in the alien world below

## The Indian Laurel

That was a place to dream
happiness was sitting on a bench
made of brick-red tiles
painted with white roses

there was no sadness
everything was forever
and the oxygen lasted
all your life

that was a place to return to
a beautiful tree under which we grew
wildly free

# Raquel on the Lovers' Bench

*She sleeps with the Angels and dreams with the Saints*
Rubén Darío

At the end of the grounds
where you see the wall
is the seat of hearts

it is a grey bench where
people in love go to kiss
and the light is furtive

I saw her for the last time there
wearing her riding boots
not knowing that soon
she would lose her life

my solitary memory
is that bitter moss
that creeps over
the cement of love

# Peacock

You open your brilliant blue fan
proud animal, exotic
and flash your thousand eyes

you glide down the gulley
we pursue your crest
like a wild pack of animals
running after the pied piper

# Scrap

(For Pedro Flores)

Beside the banana depot
brays the old truck
that used to transport goods to sell

we clamber in
play with the gear stick
and drive to the stars

we travel the universe
with our ragged crew
and a tin of biscuits

# The Gramophone

I liked to play the record
listen to the music without words
that older people enjoyed

Nipper the dog would listen
and the symphonies seemed to me
to be the work of an untamed animal

# Butterfly

When they told me the green caterpillar
would become a butterfly
I was caught under the spell of metamorphosis

and felt a shiver run down my spine
because we had no chrysalis
to hide in and evolve

# The Green Friend

When the cricket died
we put it in a matchbox
and threw earth on it

then we made a cross
and took it a rose

somebody said that maybe God
was an immense ancient insect
but we thought then
that it was only our pets that died

# A Memory

Rosario scattered the grains of corn
that she carried in her apron
and the chickens crowded round her

we went to the meadow
to play in the long grass
not suspecting that when older
the world would be barren

# The Swing

A board hangs from the tree
we cling onto the rope
and swing back and forward

we climb higher and higher
till we touch the blue sky
where nothing can stop us

# The Ants

We are not soldier ants
nor must we go in a straight line
as the worker ants do
back and forward over the bathroom tiles

we are queens with no offspring
we did not want our children
to mix with the worms

## The Patio

The pink bracts creep up
the old wall
carrying tiny white flowers

the bougainvillea flares up
and offers us flowers
that remind us of origami

one day the flowers will be paper
they will not smell of country
and we will burn them

# Dandy the Dog

I want to go on being a dog
curling up in the garden
lost in idle thought

running after you to play with you
licking you and guarding you

I want to be this animal
noble in character
and white splashed skin

a quiet animal
a romantic dog

# The Rocking Chair

It was in the bedroom at the end of the corridor
where there were spider webs
and leftover pieces of other lives

every now and then it would rock
its wood creaking remembering
someone who smoked a pipe

nobody touched it
nor moved it from where it was
it rocked sacred air

# Kneeler

The cat perches on it
and scratches the brocade
where knees rest to pray

it is a dark piece of furniture
that secrets the sins
of someone who loved God

# Spice Rack

We will cry like the fake pepper tree
when we cannot stand in its shade
and our tears will be made of resin

we will sit on a bench
looking for red berries
in an imaginary garden

a guard will come
and tell us we are crazy
and handcuff our nostalgia

# Black Earth

The house was surrounded by gravel
that shone like volcanic rock
and crunched underfoot as we trod carefully

we were surrounded by earth
small stones that possessed us
and mud where people from times past had trod

## The Country

When you took my hand
we walked through the poppies
and puffed dandelion seeds into the sky

we weren't to know dear papá
that one day we would cling to one another
to cross fields of thorns

# The Grape Harvest

In September we would go to the vineyard
and tread the harvest

it was a scarlet liquid
that slumbered drowsily in barrels
until it entered our souls

I will steep my hands in wine
to uncover your deepest hidden self

# Mirage

We looked at our reflections in the well
framed within the moss-covered walls
and our reflections were caught
for our whole lives

deep down below flitted
from time to time
a watery shadow

# Truth or Dare

They loved that the twig
ended up in the hand
of someone who was asked
to tell the truth
make someone climb a wall
or kiss you on your lips

# The Fishbowl

Sometimes time would disappear
watching it flicking slender fins to and fro
the goldfish with the veil-tail

in the crystal ball
thoughts drifted
and were caught in the gravel at the bottom

# Dromedary

Often, I felt
like that big animal
hairy and clumsily peculiar

I did not feel like I belonged
nor did I like to be taken
to see the Three Wise Men, pass by

I was a foreigner with no language
and a hump full of unknowns

# The Camera

You would take it everywhere with you
slung from your shoulder
as if it were part of you

you took a photo of us with the white
dove sitting on the coloured bench or in clouds of dust
when we ran sack races

all your photos, mamá
bring back times past
when we were unique

# The Porch

Twilight crept in over
the wooden benches
and the dalmation-spotted wall

the coffee pot was on the table
and the tray of sweet treats
reserved for special days

a bird landed
pecked at the crumbs
while you took a photo
and gifted us the future

# The Tricycle

It took us to the limit
where there was a steep fall
filled with prickly pear cacti

You told us not to go there
that it was dangerous to tempt fate
but we pedalled back like crazy
time and time again to the abyss

# The Hideaway

Up the slope you came
to a cave for dogs
where the spiders wove their webs

we did not want to go in
it smelt of ogre's feet
and a monster's foul breath

# The Fenced-off Area

> *I will return to my world of keys without memory*
> Benjamín Prado

I have also felt like this
surrounded by a fence
as if I were a potato patch

some day I will be grey
you will bite my flesh
and I will be your food

# The Excursion

We used to go with a hamper
and we would spread our blanket
in the shade of a tree

the afternoon tasted of chocolate
on milk bread
and happiness faded away
like a mechanical toy slows down
when its batteries are dying

# Crying

My tears were resin
that stuck to my fingers
and accumulated sadness

sadness was trapped
in a glass droplet
like a butterfly in amber

# Fear

We woke up at the sound
an unknown voice
the sound of a footstep in pine needles

we sank in the hay
that filled the mattress
and the ghosts slipped through the door

they were large and with no eyes
and they swallowed us up
in one go

# Shifting Sand

At the bottom of the gulley
not even goats can get there
and only agaves grow

they told us there were shifting sands
that swallowed up kids
and pets

nobody went anywhere near there
the earth is hungry
for tortured souls

## Cot Bed

We would climb up onto the mattress
striped red and white
and jump for joy

at night you would whisper
wicked tales to her
so you could hug her
and embrace her heart

# The Cage

Beside the cows
there were budgies trapped
between wooden bars

they looked like porcelain figures
a species from another forest
still as statues

we did not know that if we let them go
they would disappear forever
in the untameable sky

# The Car called Bang

(For my brother Daniel Rodríguez)

> *Antidepressants are like pesticides.*
> *And the end of fairy tales is always a lie.*
> *so that no kid commits suicide.*
>
> Joan Margarit

My brother had a car with wings
A magic car that flew around and above the world

the whole family piled in
father mother boy and girl
and I thought that we
would be invincible
like those plastic toys

# The Angel

It was an invisible being
with white wings
and an innocent smile

it caught you in the air
to lay you down on the hay
before you split your head open
on the rusty old cart

# Flower of the World

At the entrance, there were two flowerpots
with blue hortensias
that smelt of other times

the round bushes
led us to the lounge
where the furniture was all antique
and your life a portrait in black and white

# The Cradle

It rocked alone
there was no-one inside
after so many children

it was now an antique piece
that groaned in the darkness
like an old rattle

## The Piñata

They hung it in the hall
a hexagon made of cardboard
decorated with fairy tale characters

someone blindfolded hit it with the broom
and out burst trumpets and streamers
whistles masks toy dolls and yoyos

before it burst
we kept to our places
like tamed wild strawberries
in the jelly topping on a cake

# The Happy Birthday

Mamá snapped us happy
sitting around the table
blowing out the candles

we were all smiling
in the old-fashioned dining room
unaware that one day
we would have to search for happiness
in photos kept in an old box

# The Garden

There was a little space
with daisy borders
and some dry grass

we played in the earth
we stored the pebbles
and we dug out hides

we liked the mud
because we did not know
that one day it would swallow us up

# Love is a Bitch

We heard an orgy
of barking and dogs fighting
at the bottom of the gulley

it was as if they were hurling stones around and
they bit one another fiercely but
they were only making love
like crazy animals on heat

# The Secret

I will believe you if you promise
then you will have to swear it
and if all you say is true
take a rose thorn
and we will seal it with blood

# The Daisy

He loves me a lot a little not at all
we still do not know who
we are pulling the petals off for
but back then love was platonic
eternal lovers and prophetic petals

# The Larder

It was a small damp room
with a fridge run on a dynamo
and a sideboard full of drawers

in each drawer somebody sighed
some ancestor that was sinking
into the traces of flour
and the stench of vinegar

# The Barn

The cows ate from the trough
and licked the water as if it were their calves
and allowed themselves to be milked

I did not like to see them tied up
nor did I understand why things
were the way they were

sometimes goddesses
walk on carpets of dung

# The Wall

Someone had to face the wall
they turned and everyone froze
to one, two, three, can't catch me

behind the trellis our parents
attacked one other with clubs and spades
in a cloud of strong tobacco

# Ghost

They said it was a shadow
all in our imagination
or someone returning

it was a white figure
that walked through the pine trees
and sometimes wept

they also claimed it was a madman
who escaped in his pyjamas
from an uninhabited sanatorium

# The Future

At that time that I still do not understand
I search the farm to find albeit momentarily
your strong figure among the poppies

I run when something moves
ready to sink
forever in your body

and I embrace the air you no longer breathe
I throw myself to the ground and call
you like a sad dog with no owner

# Forfeits

The room is in darkness
each of us in our hiding places
I hide in a corner

ready or not here I come
they discover someone
recognise them and say their name

they touched your face
I do not know if when you die
you also choose a spectre

# Sunday

Behind the pines they sacrifice wood
for the grill and burn alcohol
that chars the skin of the peppers

papá and the men talk laugh
among the smoke clouds
and return glowing to us
like the charcoal embers in the fire
glow when they are eating them up inside

## Doggone Flowers

The roses anthuriums and daisies
were inseparable animals
that howled together at your death

every now and again they revive
I stab my fingers with their thorns
and they crown my thoughts

## Shooting Star

You show me a meteor
that swiftly disappears
and I can make a wish

you take a tiny eyelash of mine
we press it with our fingers
and I make a wish because it sticks to me

I wish that all the stars disappear
for you to return from that place
that someone called heaven

# Blind Man's Buff

Many times after
I had my eyes blindfolded
and span round and round till dizzy

I even blinded myself so as not to see
your protruding cheekbones
your imminent death
and continue to spin round and round
caught up in that natural joy surrounding
the innocent children we were

# Cross Stitch

It took me forever to finish the picture
of the girl playing
with the cat in the country
and the multi-coloured ball

how many crosses will the needle sew
in the canvas of my soul
until I finish the incomplete drawing
of my imperfect existence

# The Palm Tree

It stands alone and strong
in the middle of nowhere
a tropical beauty

its trunk survives my dreams
although some nights
on its back may fall
an undesirable rat skin

# The Extra-Terrestrial Doll

I took it everywhere with me
like an inseparable friend
and earthly confidante

when I pressed its button
its finger came alight
and signalled to another planet

that orange light fires
the primitive emotions
of my strange generation

# The Meadow

The herd of cows goes back to the grass
where it is bred in the shadow
of an inhumane world

I want to go where there is pasture
that nourishes some doctrine
find faith again
in that rational animal
that battles against the world

## Rose Garden

> *Rose,*
> *if you did not have a stem,*
> *you would rise like an angel*
>
> Eduardo Lizalde

When a rose was wilting
we thought it was sleeping
like the princess in the fairy tale
and we would put it in water

then much later
we understood that the rose
was never going to wake
and the thorns crept up around us
there where death hurts

## Bitter Sweet

Now I am melting
like the chocolate of those
umbrellas wrapped in cellophane
and that I kept in the glove compartment

everything is sticky with a sad substance
that leaves its dark trace
of somebody that is disintegrating

# Hour Glass

You turned it over
and pink dust fell
into a silent dune

while something was cooking
the minutes of the egg sifted through
or the noodles boiled tender

what we did not know then
was that our time would fall
like a handful of heavenly earth
and crash like a satellite
into the dust of the galaxy

# The Sky/Heaven

When the clouds are tinged orange
violet pink reddish
the Virgin Mary is ironing

someone finds a red insect
and places it on his hand and says
spread your wings and go with God

in heaven are the good
those we love
but nobody can touch the sky
unless it crashes round your ears

TRANSLATION: MARGARET HART ROBERTSON

# Silvia Rodríguez

I was born in Las Palmas de Gran Canaria in the Canary Islands on 1st April 1970, that is on April Fools' Day for people in the English-speaking world. My translator into English, Margaret Hart, was also born in April a long time before but on the 7th, a fact that her father reminded her of every birthday as, in the past, income tax was paid on 1st April (from there, the April Fools) and he did not get a rebate that year because she was born late (due on the 1st). So, I suppose we were meant to be working together.

*Marabulla*, the original name in Canary Island Spanish for the children's game of Forfeits, always sounded to me like *maravilla*, a marvel, and so that mysterious connection between the two words led me to revisit my relation to language, to the past and to pull on that ball of used wool, unravelling the text of my life that had been torn apart. My father was a great admirer of Sylvie Vartan and so he called me Silvia. I think people's roots, reasons, details and dreams are important. *Marabulla* or Forfeits is a book that rescues moments from the past, above all from childhood with all of its traumas, fears, impressions and personal scenarios: the Indian laurel, a swing, an old truck, a water-tank full of green water or an extra-terrestrial doll, E.T. that stole the heart of a strange generation. These are poems of rebellion against the cruel curse of knowing that we are to lose what and whom we love most. There are poems like "Baby Bird",

"Butterfly", "Dromedary", "Dandy Dog" or others that talk of furniture that take us back to other times, like the kneeler or the rocking chair. They are an attempt to come to terms with melancholy and nostalgia, with the insufferable pain of our ephemeral time on earth. The title refers to a game we played in the Canary Islands when we were little that we called *Marabulla sin bulla* (all together but told apart, no time like the present). Someone was made to go into a dark room where the other kids were all hiding. The kid that entered had to feel his or her way around in the dark until they found someone and then try to identify them, give them a name. If they got it right, they stayed in the room in the dark and the other person had to leave. As I say in the poem that offers the title to this collection of poems, I do not know if when you die, you also get to choose a spectre: a forfeit. So, this is about revisiting and re-creating childhood, innocence and happiness as seen from maturity, from the perspective of the present, with all of its bittersweet taste, the bitter flavour of time that has gone, and of the new forebodings that await us. The shadow of the loss of innocence, of illusions and fantasies hangs over the poems like a pall. All the photos that my mother took of us as kids tell the same story, of the time that we were unrepeatable, unique: the marvel or *marabulla* of another time.

I live in the city where I was born, in this ultra-peripheral region of Europe where everything is much more remote and invisible. The Canary Islands have always been strongly influenced by the UK, with strong historical links, above all with England, with London (The Canary Wharf). The British lived and worked here, at home on the island of Gran Canaria, and left their imprint economically and socioculturally, even on the language. Just one example of the many is that kids here call cake, *queque* instead of the Spanish word *bizcocho*. I am convinced that poetry as I feel it and suffer it survives against all odds and that it needs to live and to stir that other animal called human beings, to awaken them. The poetry that means something to me has no bounds and I work in that abyss by way of vocation, as a calling. In the words of Gabriel Celaya, poetry is a weapon loaded with future. Or in the words of Pedro Flores, poetry is an old woman who waits for a happy gentleman who adores her without seeing her.

I was wrong when I thought as a kid that my family and our friends would live forever like the plastic toys of the characters in the film Chitty Chitty Bang Bang that sat in my brother Daniel's magic flying car.